sun-dried tomatoes

Sun-dried Tomatoes

Ethel Brennan

Georgeanne Brennan

Illustrated by Jack Molloy

CHRONICLE BOOKS

SAN FRANCISCO

Acknowledgments

Special thanks to Short Night Farm,
Frances Andrews and Nigel Walker, Jane's Organic Acres,
Stone Free Farms, Jesse Cool, Katie Thompson,
Leslie Jonath, and Bill LeBlond.

Library of Congress Cataloging-in-Publication Data available.

Printed in Hong Kong.

ISBN 0-8118-0627-8

Book design by Sarah Bolles

Distributed in Canada by Raincoast Books
8680 Cambie Street, Vancouver, B.C. V6P 6M9

10   9   8   7   6   5   4   3   2   1

Chronicle Books
275 Fifth Street
San Francisco, CA 94103

Table of Contents

Introduction

The origin of the tomato lies in South America. Tomato seeds were first carried from the New World to Europe in the early sixteenth century on Spanish ships loaded with cargoes of gold and other plunder, along with the seeds, tubers, and cuttings of other exotic plants. By the early 1600s the tomato plant, whose fruit was called *pomme d'amour* (love apple) by the French, had become a popular curiosity that was grown primarily as an ornamental. A member of the Solanaceae family, which also contains the deadly nightshade, the tomato was scrutinized by northern Europeans for its edibility into the nineteenth century.

It was in Italy, though, sitting there patiently with its pasta, garlic, and olive oil, that the tomato found early culinary acceptance, and was used in a wide range of dishes. The Italians, as well as other Mediterraneans, were accustomed to using their warm, dry climate to preserve a number of dietary staples, such as figs, dates, and grapes, so as fresh tomatoes became associated with the local cuisines, so did sun-dried tomatoes.

The actual drying techniques vary from region to region. For example, in Sicily, tomatoes are traditionally sliced and laid out on tile roof tops to dry. On the Greek island of Khios in the Aegean off Turkey's west coast, they are strung on threads and hung in the sun. But despite such differences, the results are the same.

Although dried tomatoes have a long culinary history in the Mediterranean, their popularity in the United States is a relatively new phenomenon. About fifteen years ago, olive oil-packed dried tomatoes imported primarily from Italy and Greece started appearing in gourmet food shops, and restaurants began to feature them on their menus. Pizzas were topped with slices of the imported tomatoes, fresh goat cheese, and basil and baked to a crispy gold in wood-fired ovens. Pastas were dressed with sun-dried tomato pesto, and bits of the deep, red tomatoes were added to salads and soups. The United States had discovered a new version of its most popular vegetable.

As the enthusiasm for using dried tomatoes increased, so did the demand for them. Commercial drying yards started buying part of the tomato crop of farmers who cultivated large tracts of land. Smaller tomato growers began experimenting with drying a portion of their own crops, and today we find domestic dried tomatoes sold side by side with the imports, either oil-packed or dry, in bulk or packaged.

Dried tomatoes, whether imported or domestic, have a highly concentrated taste and intense color that bring a versatile range of visual and flavor possibilities to the kitchen. A silver dollar sized piece of a dried Red Roma tomato cooked in a golden onion soup turns the soup a rich amber-orange and imbues the onions themselves with a subtle hint of tomato. Yet, bits of the same dried tomato added to a cream-based pasta sauce just before serving allows the sauce to retain its pristine ivory color while giving a surprising burst of tomato taste.

A Short Guide to Dried Tomatoes

Historically, it has been the Roma types and other meaty, high-solid, red paste tomatoes, that have been commercially dried. These are generally labeled simply as "Dried Tomatoes." While the Red Roma type dominates the dried tomato market, there is a movement among trendsetting chefs and cooks to use specialty tomatoes in dried form. And consequently, dried tomatoes with specific varietal labeling are beginning to appear in some innovative markets.

All tomatoes can be dried, and there exist dozens of attractive and unusual tomatoes to be discovered. Their tastes range from quite sweet to highly acidic, with various underlying hints of berry, citrus, smoke, and other flavors. Since it may be difficult to find specialty tomatoes already dried, try purchasing them fresh at farmers' or specialty produce markets, and drying your own.

Early Girl — medium, round, reddish-orange tomato; sweet distinctive tomato flavor; cut in slices or quarters to dry

Evergreen — a medium to large tomato with bright green meat and a greenish yellow streaked skin; cut in slices or quarters to dry; dark olive when dried; tart, slightly smoked flavor

Great White — large, meaty tomato with an almost opalescent skin that covers ivory flesh; cut in slices to dry; light yellow when dried; flavor well balanced between sweet and acidic

Green Grape — small tomato with greenish-gold skin and green flesh; cut in halves to dry; golden brown when dried; pronounced sweet flavor

Green Zebra — large golf-ball shaped tomato with gold and green striped skin and bright green flesh; cut in halves or quarters to dry; golden brown when dried; balanced flavor

Jubilee — medium, round, golden-yellow tomato; cut in halves, quarters, or slices to dry; rusty gold when dried; mildly sweet flavor

Marvel Stripe — large, pumpkin-shaped tomato with pinkish-yellow skin and golden flesh with bright rose marbling throughout core; cut in slices or eighths to dry; honey yellow with burnished-rose overtones when dried; sweetly tart flavor with a touch of berry

Red Currant — very small, cherry tomato type; may be dried whole or cut in halves; sweet-tart flavor

Red Pear — small, pear-shaped cherry tomato type; cut in halves to dry; slightly more acidic than the Yellow Pear

Red Roma — the classic dried tomato; medium-sized and oval shaped; cut in halves or quarters to dry; acidic tomato flavor

Sungold — a tiny, gold, cherry tomato type; cut in halves to dry; golden skin and tart flavor

Sweet 100s — small, cherry tomato type; cut in halves to dry; very sweet, fruity flavor

Yellow Pear — small, pear-shaped cherry tomato type; cut in halves to dry; sweet flavor

Purchasing Dried Tomatoes

When shopping for dried tomatoes, try to choose those to which no salt or sulphur has been added. Sulphur, used primarily to prevent browning during drying, can change the flavor of the tomatoes. Salt is sometimes added to aid in color retention and to speed up the drying process by drawing out liquid. Make sure to taste the dried tomatoes before cooking with them so that your dish will not be spoiled by overly salty tomatoes.

If you are buying dried tomatoes from bulk bins or jars, try to sample them before buying. The taste should be clean and sharp, not stale and dusty, and the texture should be leathery, not dry and hard. Oil-packed tomatoes are more supple, but they will have absorbed some oil and will bring it to the cooking. When shopping for oil-packed dried tomatoes, pay close attention to their color. If the oil and tomatoes have a cloudy or muddy appearance, the tomatoes are breaking down and have become too soft.

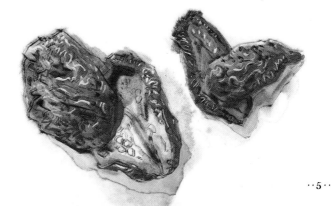

Home-Drying Tomatoes

As a rule, when a fresh tomato is dried, its original flavor becomes more pronounced. Therefore, for the tastiest dried tomatoes, it is important to use the freshest vine-ripened tomatoes available.

There are three basic methods for home-drying tomatoes. They can be dried in the sun, in a dehydrator, or in a conventional oven. Large tomatoes should be cut into thin slices crosswise, quartered from stem to bottom without severing the sections completely, or cut into wedges. Small, cherry-type tomatoes, such as Yellow Pear, Sweet 100s, and Red Currant, need to be cut only in half.

Sun-Drying

Simple drying racks can be made out of cotton-nylon mesh stretched across wooden frames. Old window screens work well, but the screening should be replaced with plastic-coated or other nonmetal screening. Because galvanized metal and aluminum screens can react with the acid in the tomatoes, these materials should be avoided.

To begin, place the tomato pieces on the racks, skin-side down. Because air circulation is essential to successful drying, leave space between each piece. Place the racks in full sun. At night, bring the tomato-filled racks inside or otherwise protect them from dew or other moisture.

Drying time can take anywhere from three days to a week, depending upon the size and thickness of the tomato pieces. A dried tomato is ready when its texture is leathery and pliable. If the tomato is sticky it still contains too much moisture. A light saltwater solution can be basted over the tomato slices before drying to preserve the tomato color. Beware, however, that the saltiness will remain.

Oven-Drying

For oven-drying, use slices of tomatoes one-eighth-inch to one-quarter-inch in width, or cherry-type tomatoes. Preheat the oven to 150 degrees F. Line baking sheets with aluminum foil, and place the tomatoes, not touching, in a single layer. Put in the oven. Drying time will take between seven and twenty-four hours, depending upon the juiciness of the tomatoes and the thickness of the slices. Leave the oven door slightly ajar and bake the tomatoes until they are leathery and dry. Reverse the racks from top to bottom halfway through the drying process and check them often during the last few hours. Because very sweet tomatoes will begin to caramelize, they are subject to burning and need careful surveying.

There are numerous brands and styles available, and each comes with its own specific instructions for drying foods. Tomatoes dried in dehydrators generally tend to be more uniform in shape and consistent in color than sun-dried or oven-dried tomatoes.

Storage of Dried Tomatoes

Once the tomatoes are dried, store them in airtight jars, plastic bags or containers, and keep them in a cool, dry, dark place for up to a year. Dried tomatoes can also be frozen or packed in olive oil in glass jars. Use the simple recipe below to pack your own tomatoes, either purchased or home-dried, in oil.

ingredients:
- 25 dried tomatoes
- 2 cups boiling water
- 1½ to 2 cups first cold-press olive oil
- 1 pint-sized glass jar

optional ingredients:
- Fresh rosemary sprigs
- Fresh thyme sprigs
- Bay leaves

Soak the tomatoes in the boiling water for 2 to 4 minutes, just long enough to soften the skins. Drain the water and pat the tomatoes dry. Put them in the canning jar. Pour the olive oil over the tomatoes, covering them completely. If you wish to season the olive oil, add a few sprigs of fresh herbs or several bay leaves. The oil-packed tomatoes will keep up to 6 months. Store in a cool, dark place or in the refrigerator.

MAKES 1 PINT.

Cooking with Dried Tomatoes

Although good-quality dried tomatoes can be eaten as one would a dried apricot or other fruit, they are more commonly used in cooking. If tomatoes are not stored in olive oil, they generally require rehydration in a liquid, such as water, broth, or milk. During this process the tomato becomes supple and the liquid intensely flavored. When dried tomatoes are rehydrated, the liquid can then be used to cook rice or to enrich a soup or sauce, adding both flavor and color. Unless they are going to be pureed, the dried tomatoes, either before or after rehydration, should be minced or finely chopped because larger pieces may by too chewy or too overpowering in a dish. Using the mezzaluna, the two-handled, half-moon knife that is common in Italian cooking, makes this task quick and easy.

It is not always necessary, however, to rehydrate dried tomatoes before using them. If you want a more subtle flavor or color, add the minced or chopped tomatoes directly to your salads, soups, bread doughs, omelets, stews or sauces.

Dried tomatoes packed in oil are not only already rehydrated but also provide a ready-made flavored olive oil to use in vinaigrettes, to drizzle over crusts of bread, or to add to warm vegetables. However, because the quality of the oil-packed dried tomatoes is so dependent on the quality of the oil used, you may choose to pack your own in a first, cold press olive oil of your choice.

Mezzaluna

Soups

and

Salads

Dried Tomato

AND GINGER SEVICHE

Nothing could be simpler to make than this seviche. The acid in the lemon juice "cooks" the raw, minced fish, leaving it moist and tender. Seviche may be eaten as a salad or served as a topping for crisp tostadas, as it is most commonly eaten in the coastal provinces of Mexico. For a pleasing flavor variation, try using a specialty dried tomato such as the Green Grape or the tiny Sungold variety.

Gently mix the cod, lemon juice, ginger, and dried tomato and let stand for 10 minutes. Add the cilantro and shallot and refrigerate until chilled, about 1 hour.

SERVES 3.

¼ *pound lingcod or other firm white*
   fish, finely diced
2 *tablespoons fresh lemon juice, about*
   1 lemon
1 *teaspoon grated fresh ginger*
1 *tablespoon minced dried tomatoes,*
   about 3 halves
1 *tablespoon coarsely chopped cilantro*
1 *shallot, minced*

Roasted New Potatoes

WITH BASIL AND DRIED TOMATOES

Rubbing the potatoes with olive oil and chopped fresh herbs before roasting them crisps their skins and gives them a robust flavor. This salad is at its most flavorful made and served when the potatoes are still warm from the oven.

Preheat the oven to 425 degrees F. Place the potatoes in a glass dish or roasting pan and coat completely with the vegetable oil. Generously sprinkle the thyme, ½ teaspoon pepper, and 1 teaspoon of the salt over the potatoes. Roast the potatoes for 45 minutes. Allow them to cool slightly and cut them into halves or quarters.

To make the vinaigrette, combine the olive oil from the tomatoes, the remaining salt and pepper, and the vinegar, and mix well. In a large salad bowl combine the potatoes, basil, tomatoes, and the vinaigrette. Season with extra salt or pepper if needed.

SERVES 6.

20 new red potatoes, about 1¾ pounds
2 tablespoons light vegetable oil
1 tablespoon fresh thyme, minced, about 4 sprigs
1 teaspoon freshly cracked pepper
1½ teaspoons salt
2 tablespoons olive oil from dried tomatoes
1 teaspoon red wine vinegar
¼ cup chopped fresh basil
8 finely chopped oil-packed dried tomatoes

Dried Tomatoes, Feta,

AND ROASTED PEPPER SALAD

The olive oil, colored and flavored by the dried tomatoes that were packed in it, makes a rich base for the vinaigrette that brings together the quintessential tastes of Greece.

2 sweet red peppers

5 to 6 oil-packed dried tomatoes, coarsely chopped

¼ pound feta cheese, crumbled

½ cup black olives, preferably Mediterranean-type

2 small cucumbers, peeled and thinly sliced

¼ cup pine nuts

1 teaspoon fresh thyme, minced, about 4 sprigs

½ teaspoon freshly cracked pepper

1 tablespoon olive oil

1 teaspoon balsamic vinegar

To roast peppers: Scorch the peppers over a gas flame or in a broiler until the skins blacken. Place charred peppers in a plastic bag while still hot and let stand for 5 minutes. Remove the peppers from the bag, run them under cold water, rub off the burned skins, and remove the seeds. Slice into ¼-inch strips.

In a medium bowl, combine the tomatoes, roasted peppers, feta cheese, olives, cucumbers, pine nuts, thyme, and pepper. In a separate bowl mix together the oil and vinegar. Toss into salad.

SERVES 4 TO 5.

Lentil Salad

WITH DRIED TOMATOES

This aromatic salad of lentils, olive oil, garlic, and dried tomatoes is ideal for picnics, or to keep on hand as a snack or as a spread for sandwiches.

Rinse the lentils several times under cold water. Bring the lentils and the water to a boil. Reduce the heat to low and simmer, uncovered, until tender, about 40 minutes. Drain any excess water from the lentils. In a bowl combine the lentils with the remaining ingredients. Chill for 30 minutes before serving.

SERVES 4 TO 6.

6 cups water

1 cup dried green lentils

1 teaspoon salt

8 oil-packed dried tomatoes, minced

1 clove garlic, minced

3 tablespoons olive oil from the tomatoes

Yellow Onion Soup

WITH PARMESAN AND GRUYÈRE CRUST

Imagine a gratinéed French onion soup that originated in the heartland of Italy instead of northern France and you will get a sense of how dried tomatoes transform this version of a culinary classic.

4 tablespoons butter

3 cups thinly sliced yellow onion

2 cloves garlic, minced

1 teaspoon dried thyme

3 cups vegetable or other broth

3 cups water

15 to 20 dried tomatoes, finely chopped

1/2 teaspoon salt

4 to 6 thick slices stale French bread or
    other hearty bread such as rye

1/2 cup shredded Parmesan cheese

1/2 cup grated Gruyère cheese

1 tablespoon chopped fresh oregano

1/2 teaspoon freshly ground black pepper

In a medium saucepan, melt the butter over low heat. Add the onion, garlic, and thyme. Raise the heat slightly and cook, stirring occasionally, until the onion is translucent, about 15 minutes. Add the vegetable broth, raise the heat to high, and bring to a boil. Add the water and the dried tomatoes and boil for 15 minutes. Remove the soup from the heat and let stand for 15 minutes. Add salt to taste.

Transfer the soup to a ceramic or glass baking dish. Top with a single layer of bread slices and cover with the Parmesan and Gruyère cheeses. Bake at 350 degrees F for about 20 minutes until golden brown. Sprinkle fresh oregano and pepper on top and serve immediately.

SERVES 4.

Chilled Soup

OF DRIED TOMATOES AND FRESH VEGETABLES

Cool, fresh vegetables of summer are combined with the intense flavor of oil-packed tomatoes. The result is a delightful cold soup that is perfect for a warm, summer evening.

Coarsely chop the cucumbers, tomatoes, and red peppers. Pulse them in a blender or food processor with the lemon juice until just blended but still chunky. Transfer mixture to a glass or ceramic bowl and stir in the garlic 1½ tablespoons of the cilantro, dried tomatoes, salt and pepper. Chill for at least ½ hour. Serve in individual bowls and garnish with the remaining cilantro.

SERVES 4.

1½ cucumbers, peeled

2 large, firm, ripe tomatoes, peeled

1 sweet red pepper, seeds removed

Juice of one lemon

1 clove garlic, minced

2 tablespoons coarsely chopped cilantro

6 to 8 oil-packed dried tomatoes

½ teaspoon salt

1 teaspoon freshly ground black pepper

Classic White Bean Soup

WITH DRIED TOMATOES

Little else chases away a winter chill as effectively as a hearty soup. This soup combines the full-bodied texture of white beans with winter savory and grated celery root, and absorbs the pale orange hue of dried tomatoes.

2 cups dried Great Northern white beans

3 ½ quarts water

1 tablespoon plus ½ teaspoon salt

1 bay leaf

12 dried tomatoes, minced

½ onion chopped, about ¼ cup

1 tablespoon butter

¾ cup grated celery root

1 clove garlic, minced

1 teaspoon freshly ground pepper

1 tablespoon minced fresh winter savory

Put the dried beans in a large soup or stock pot and cover them with the water. Add one tablespoon of salt and the bay leaf and bring to a boil. Reduce the heat to low and simmer for 2 to 2½ hours, or until the beans are tender. When the beans are done, they should still have about 5 or 6 cups of liquid left. If not, add some additional water.

When the beans are tender, add the tomato and onion. Cover and simmer for 20 minutes. While the beans are cooking, melt the butter in a small skillet over medium heat.

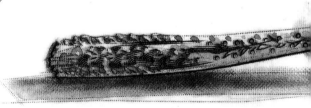

Add the celery root and sauté for another 2 to 3 minutes. Add this mixture, along with the remaining salt, the pepper, and half the winter savory, to the beans. Cover the soup and simmer for 10 minutes until the flavors have melded.

Purée approximately 1 cup of the soup in a food processor or blender, and then stir it back into the soup along with the remaining winter savory.

SERVES 8.

Entrées

Fettuccine

WITH CREAMY TOMATO MUSHROOM SAUCE

Plump, succulent oyster and button mushrooms are bound together by an ivory cream sauce with aromatic fresh herbs and enriched by a subtle tomato flavor.

3/4 cup boiling water

6 to 8 dried tomatoes

1 tablespoon olive oil

3 to 4 large cloves garlic, finely chopped

1/2 cup cold water, as needed

1 teaspoon minced fresh rosemary

1 teaspoon minced fresh thyme

10 to 12 oyster mushrooms, halved or
     quartered, depending upon size

1 cup button mushrooms, thinly sliced

2/3 to 3/4 cup heavy whipping cream

1/2 teaspoon salt

1 12-ounce package fresh fettuccine

Pour the boiling water over the dried tomatoes to rehydrate them and let stand for 5 to 10 minutes. Remove the tomatoes from the water, and set the water aside. Coarsely chop the tomatoes. In a heavy frying pan, heat the olive oil over medium heat, add the garlic, and reduce heat to low. Add the chopped tomatoes and the tomato water, stirring for 1 or 2 minutes. Begin adding the cold water a little at a time to retain moisture for the sauce. Add the fresh rosemary and thyme. Let simmer over low heat, stirring constantly to prevent burning. Toss in the

mushrooms, stirring until they become tender, about 4 to 5 minutes. Add the heavy cream and salt, reduce heat to very low, and continue to stir constantly. Let cook for another 4 to 5 minutes until sauce thickens slightly.

Meanwhile bring a large pot of salted water to a boil. Add pasta and cook until tender, about 3 to 4 minutes. Drain well and divide pasta into individual portions. Generously top with the sauce. Serve immediately.

Serves 4.

Gratinéed Italian Pancakes

This is a simple country dish made with ingredients traditionally found in Italian farm pantries, fields, and gardens. Wild greens such as chicory, dandelion, and arugula might be used in Italy, but we suggest parsley, chives, and chard, which are more readily available. However, any greens may be used as a foil for the rich taste of the dried tomatoes. A sweeter variety of dried tomato, such as the Early Girl or Jubilee works well with this recipe.

Pancakes:
1 1/4 cups milk
3/4 cup flour
2 eggs
3/4 teaspoon salt
2 tablespoons butter

In a mixing bowl, whisk the milk, flour, eggs, and salt until smooth. In an 8-inch, preferably non-stick, frying pan melt about 1 teaspoon of the butter and pour in 1/4 cup of the batter, swirling the pan quickly to create a large, thin pancake. Cook over medium heat for about 2 to 3 minutes on each side. (If you let the pancakes get too crispy, they will be difficult to fill and roll later.) Set pancakes aside and prepare the filling.

MAKES 8 PANCAKES.

Soak the dried tomatoes in the boiling water. In a frying pan, melt the butter and sauté the onion and garlic over medium heat for 2 to 3 minutes. Add the parsley and chard and cook for another 2 to 3 minutes. In a bowl, mix together the tomatoes, which will have completely absorbed the water, the onion mixture, the ricotta cheese, salt, and the pepper.

Fill each pancake with about 2 tablespoons of the filling, roll up, and place side by side in a shallow, ungreased baking dish.

Preheat the oven to 350 degrees F. Over a low heat, melt the butter and add the flour and salt, stirring constantly with a wire whisk. Raise the heat and slowly add the milk, stirring constantly. Cook until the sauce begins to thicken, about 5 minutes. Pour the sauce over the pancakes and sprinkle the teaspoon of remaining dried tomatoes over the top. Bake for 15 to 20 minutes until the top is slightly golden and the sauce is bubbly.

SERVES 4.

Filling:
½ cup dried tomatoes, minced, about 8 to 10 tomatoes (set aside 1 tablespoon for topping)
¼ cup boiling water
2 tablespoons butter
½ onion, minced
1 clove garlic, minced
⅓ cup parsley, finely chopped
2 large leaves green chard, coarsely chopped, including the whiter ribs
1 cup ricotta cheese
½ teaspoon salt
1 teaspoon freshly ground pepper

Bechamel Sauce:
2 tablespoons butter
3 tablespoons flour
½ teaspoon salt
1 cup milk

Riso With Chorizo,

AND FRESH AND DRIED TOMATOES

Topped with freshly grated Parmesan cheese and served with a salad of tender young greens, this simple dish, full of flavor and color becomes a main course.

3 cups water

³/₄ cup riso pasta

¹/₂ cup dried tomatoes, finely chopped

2 chorizo sausages, cut into ¹/₄-inch
    slices

¹/₄ cup freshly grated Parmesan

¹/₄ cup fresh Italian parsley, coarsely
    chopped

20 fresh Yellow Pear tomatoes,
    quartered

Bring the water to a boil in a medium saucepan. Add the riso and dried tomatoes and boil for about 25 to 30 minutes, until the water has been fully absorbed and the pasta is tender.

Meanwhile, cook the chorizo in a frying pan over medium heat until cooked through, about 15 minutes. In a large bowl mix together the pasta, chorizo, cheese, parsley, and yellow tomatoes.

SERVES 4 TO 6.

Mussels,

STEAMED IN TOMATO AND SAFFRON BROTH

One of the best things about steamed mussels is the broth they create as they release their salty sea juices. Spiked with saffron, dried tomato, garlic, and white wine, the broth reminds one of the flavors of the Spanish paella.

Put the butter, olive oil, onion, thyme, tomatoes, and saffron in the bottom of a stock pot or soup pot large enough to hold all the mussels. Add the mussels and pour the white wine over them. Sprinkle on the grated garlic. Cover, turn the heat to medium, and cook just until the mussels open, about 10 minutes.

Serve the mussels in soup bowls with a ladle or two of the broth.

SERVES 8.

1 tablespoon butter
1 tablespoon olive oil
¼ cup diced onions
1 tablespoon fresh thyme leaves
15 dried tomato halves
1 gram saffron
8 pounds fresh mussels in the shell,
    scrubbed, debearded
1 cup dry white wine
1 clove garlic, grated

Rock Cod

POACHED IN WHITE WINE

A fresh filet of rock cod poached in this tangy sauce of capers, white wine, and dried tomatoes will satiate even the most ravenous of appetites.

Melt the butter with the garlic over a medium heat until the butter begins to foam. Increase the heat to high and add the fish, searing it for 30 seconds on each side. Reduce the heat slightly and add the wine, deglazing the pan. Poach the fish in the wine for 2 to 3 minutes on each side. Top each fillet with the tomatoes and capers and reduce the heat to very low. Cover and let simmer for about 10 minutes adding the 2 tablespoons water if too much liquid has evaporated. Cook until fish is firm but flakes easily. Serve immediately.

SERVES 4.

1 tablespoon butter

1 clove garlic, minced

2 1½-inch filets of rock cod or other firm, white fish

½ cup white wine

½ cup dried tomatoes, minced and rehydrated in ¼ cup boiling water

1 tablespoon capers

2 tablespoons water

Summer Lamb Ragout

Although ragouts or stews usually belong to the cool seasons of fall and winter, this ragout, full of warm-weather vegetables, is wonderful on a summer night with a green salad and a glass of slightly chilled red wine.

1 tablespoon olive oil

1 large yellow onion, sliced in thin
    rounds

2 cloves garlic, minced

1/2 pound lamb shoulder, cubed

8 to 10 oil–packed dried tomatoes

3 fresh bay leaves

3 sprigs fresh thyme

1 1/2 cups water

2 yellow peppers, sliced lengthwise into
    1/2-inch-thick strips

1 red or green pepper, cut as above

1 teaspoon salt

1 to 2 teaspoons freshly ground
    black pepper

1 medium to large eggplant, coarsely
    chopped

1 small Anaheim chili, halved lengthwise

In a large pot over medium heat, heat the olive oil and add the onion, garlic, lamb, dried tomatoes, bay leaves, and thyme. Cook, stirring constantly, for 5 minutes. Add ½ cup of the water and bring to a boil. Add the peppers, another ½ cup of water, and the salt and pepper. Allow to cook down about 10 minutes.

Add the eggplant and the chili, continue to cook on medium heat about 20 minutes, and add the remaining ½ cup water. Let simmer over a low heat until the eggplant is very soft, forming a thick sauce, about 15 minutes. Serve with long-grain white or brown rice.

SERVES 4.

Lamb with Spicy Ancho Chili

AND DRIED TOMATO CRUST

A succulent boned leg of lamb is encased within a spicy sweet crust of toasted chilies, dried tomatoes, and honey to make a centerpiece dish for a special occasion. Traditional trimmings including baby carrots, parsnips, and even sweet potatoes complete this culinary extravaganza.

4-pound boned and butterflied leg of
    lamb
1 tablespoon salt
1 tablespoon black pepper
1 tablespoon fresh thyme leaves
1 tablespoon ancho chili powder
4 cloves garlic, slivered
4 dried ancho chilies
20 dried tomatoes
3/4 cup boiling water
2 mashed garlic cloves
2 tablespoons honey

Preheat oven to 350 degrees F.

Using paper towels, dry the leg of lamb. Mix together the salt, black pepper, thyme, and chili powder in a small bowl. Rub the lamb all over with the mixture. With a sharp knife, make about 20 1-inch-deep slits all over the leg of lamb. Put a sliver of garlic in each slit and set the lamb aside.

In an ungreased skillet toast the ancho chilies over medium heat. Put the ancho chilies in it. Press them down gently with the back of a wooden spoon, 1 to 2 minutes on each side. (Be careful not to burn them.) They will become supple as they warm. Remove the stems and seeds from the chilies and discard. Put the chilies in a bowl with the dried tomatoes and cover with boiling water. Let stand about 15 minutes until softened.

Pour the tomato-chili mixture, including the water, into a food processor or blender and purée. Add the garlic and honey. Process for 30 seconds, or just long enough to form a thick paste.

Place the lamb on a rack in a roasting pan just large enough to hold it. Paint the top, sides, and ends with a ½-inch-thick coating of the tomato-chili mixture. Put a meat thermometer into the thickest part of the lamb. Place the lamb in the middle of the oven. In approximately 45 minutes, or when the thermometer registers 160°, remove from oven. For medium rare, remove from the oven and let stand 10 to 15 minutes before serving. For well-done lamb, cook about 15 minutes longer or until the thermometer registers 170°.

SERVES 6 TO 8.

Seared Sirloin Strips

WITH DRIED TOMATOES AND MUSHROOMS

Tender beef strips cooked in the flavorful juices of mushrooms and dried tomatoes make a quick topping for pasta or rice.

10 dried tomatoes, minced
½ cup boiling water
1 teaspoon salt
½ pound sirloin roast cut into ¼-inch
    strips
2 tablespoons butter
2 cups whole button mushrooms
1 small onion cut into thin slices
1 tablespoon minced fresh tarragon

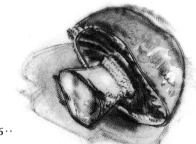

Rehydrate the tomatoes in the boiling water and set aside. Over high heat, add the salt to a heavy medium-sized frying pan. When the pan is well heated, add the sirloin strips. Sear them for 30 seconds on either side, then remove them from the pan and set aside.

Reduce the heat to low and melt 1 tablespoon of the butter and sauté the mushrooms for 3 to 4 minutes until they begin to release their juices and then set aside with the beef. To the same pan, add the remaining tablespoon of butter. Sauté the onions for 5 minutes until translucent. Add the tarragon and dried tomatoes including the water. Allow to simmer for another 3 to 4 minutes. Add the beef and mushrooms along with their juices and cook over a medium heat for 5 minutes. Serve hot with riso pasta.

SERVES 4.

Roasted Beef Shanks

WITH LEEKS AND CARROTS

This slow-cooked dish is tender and flavorful and aside from the natural juices of the beef shanks, there is no added fat or oil. Potatoes, parsnips, and squash are other vegetables that can be cooked along with the meat. Serve hot with rice, potatoes, or pasta.

Preheat oven to 400 degrees F.

Place the beef shanks in a deep roasting pan and cook in the oven for 20 minutes. If more than a tablespoon of fat melts from the beef, remove and discard. Meanwhile, boil 1 cup of the water and rehydrate the tomatoes. Set aside.

When the beef is browned, add the carrots, celery, leeks, beef broth, thyme, and the tomatoes with their water. Reduce oven to 375 degrees F. Cook for 2 hours, checking every 20 minutes to make sure the stock has not evaporated. Add the remaining 2 cups of water as needed in order to retain the moisture. The meat is done when it is tender enough to be cut with a fork and pulls easily away from the bone. Top each serving with the flavorful juices.

SERVES 3 TO 4.

2 beef shanks

3 cups water

15 dried tomatoes, minced

2 cups sliced carrots

2 cups sliced celery

2 leeks, sliced in ½-inch rounds, green
    stalks removed

1 cup beef broth

5 to 6 sprigs fresh thyme

Chicken Breasts

STUFFED WITH DRIED TOMATOES AND GOAT CHEESE

Layers of dried tomatoes, soft goat cheese, and red peppers are tucked between the skin and the meat of boned chicken breasts, and then broiled. Reminiscent of saltimbocca or chicken Kiev, it is easier to prepare and lighter to eat.

3 large, sweet red peppers

4 boned chicken breasts, small- to
  medium-sized

8 to 10 tablespoons soft goat cheese

10 oil-packed dried tomatoes, coarsely
  chopped

5 tablespoons olive oil

2 tablespoons chopped fresh thyme or
  rosemary

Preheat oven to 400 degrees F.

Roast the peppers over a gas fire, under a broiler, or on a barbecue until the skins blacken. Place the peppers in a plastic bag while they are still hot. Close the bag and let stand for 5 to 10 minutes. Remove the peppers, rinse them under cold, running water, and rub off the skins. Slice the peppers into ¼-inch-thick strips, and set aside.

Partially separate the skin of the chicken breasts, creating a pocket between the meat and the skin. Make a lengthwise slit in the meat about 1 inch deep and 2 inches long, creating a second pocket. In each pocket, make a layer of dried

tomatoes, goat cheese, and roasted pepper. Generously coat each breast with olive oil (about 1½ teaspoons per breast). Place the filled breasts on a grill pan or a roasting pan with the skins up. Sprinkle the tops with generous amounts of thyme or rosemary. Bake at 400 degrees F for 30 minutes, until the skins are crispy and the juices run clear.

SERVES 4.

Gratin of Chard

AND DRIED TOMATOES

Chard, a full-flavored green, lends itself to the Mediterranean flavors of olive oil, dried tomatoes, and garlic. Although the chard can simply be steamed and then tossed with the oil-packed dried tomatoes, the final flourish of topping it with bread crumbs and an extra drizzle of olive oil heightens the flavors.

2 large bunches of green chard
1 teaspoon olive oil
1 clove garlic, crushed
2 tablespoons olive oil from dried
    tomatoes
1 teaspoon salt
8 oil-packed dried tomatoes, finely
    chopped
2 tablespoons bread crumbs

Chop the chard, including the white stalks, into strips about 2 inches long and 1 inch wide. Steam the white stalks for about 2 minutes, add the greens and steam for a total of 5 minutes.

Rub the bottom and sides of a shallow baking dish with the olive oil and crushed garlic. In a mixing bowl, combine the chard, 1 tablespoon of the olive oil from the tomatoes, salt, and the oil-packed dried tomatoes. Fold the ingredients together gently and put into the baking dish. Sprinkle bread crumbs over the top and drizzle with the remaining olive oil. Broil until bread crumbs become a golden brown, about 5 minutes. Serve hot or at room temperature.

SERVES 8.

Breads and Pastas

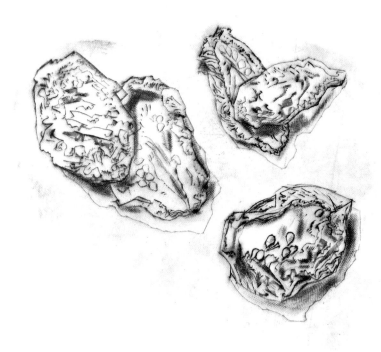

Sweet White Corn

AND DRIED TOMATO SPOON BREAD

Kernels of fresh, sweet corn, cut off the cob and folded with dried tomatoes into a mixture of milk, corn meal, and egg, make a golden soufflé-like bread. The tangy flavor of dried Red Currant or Red Pear tomatoes enhance this dish.

Preheat oven to 350 degrees F. Using half the butter, grease a baking dish.

In a large mixing bowl, combine the corn meal and boiling water, and let stand for 5 minutes. Add the fresh corn, dried tomatoes, spinach, salt, pepper and egg yolks, and mix well with a wooden spoon. Fold in the egg whites. Pour the mixture into the greased baking dish and dot the top with the remaining butter. Bake for 40 minutes until golden brown and a knife inserted into the middle comes out clean.

SERVES 6 TO 8.

1 tablespoon butter

1 cup yellow corn meal

1 1/2 cups boiling water

2 cups of fresh white corn kernels, about 2 ears

1/2 cup dried tomatoes, finely chopped

1/2 cup fresh spinach, coarsely chopped

1/2 teaspoon salt

1 teaspoon freshly cracked pepper

3 egg yolks, well beaten

5 egg whites, whipped to soft peaks

Dried Tomato

AND GREEN OLIVE FOCACCIA

Yeast, olive oil, and flour are the basis of this simple peasant bread that becomes softly imbued both in flavor and color by the dried tomato bits. This focaccia is virtually foolproof, even for inexperienced bread makers. Serve it as you would any other bread. Sliced in half crosswise and then filled with roast pork, Italian peppers, and grilled onions, it makes an exceptional sandwich, especially when thickly spread with aioli. Try using dried Evergreen or Marvel Stripe tomatoes in this bread.

2 packages dry yeast

1½ cups warm water

12 oil-packed dried tomatoes, chopped

4½ cups all-purpose flour

¾ cup olive oil

½ cup chopped green olives

1 teaspoon salt

In a large mixing bowl, dissolve the yeast in ½ cup of the warm water and let stand for 5 minutes. Add to the yeast 4 cups of the flour, the remaining 1 cup water, the tomatoes, ¼ cup of the olive oil, the olives, and the salt. Mix until a dough forms. The dough will be soft and sticky. Cover with a damp kitchen towel. Let rise for 1½ hours.

Punch down the dough and remove from the mixing bowl. Using another ¼ cup of the olive oil, coat the sides of the mixing bowl and roll the dough in it, covering it with olive oil. Let dough rise a second time for 20 to 30 minutes.

Preheat the oven to 400 degrees F. Using half of the remaining olive oil, coat the bottom and sides of a 12-by-18-inch or other medium-sized baking sheet. Dust a board with the remaining flour. Punch down the dough and flatten it out by stretching equally from all sides. Lay the dough flat on the baking sheet and baste the top with all the remaining olive oil. Bake for 20 minutes or until the focaccia is a golden brown color. Cut into squares or thin slices.

Savory Bread Pudding

WITH FRESH HERBS AND FONTINA CHEESE

We tend to think of bread puddings as sweet, but when milk-soaked bread is combined with salt, pepper, fresh herbs, and cheese, the result is akin to a main-dish soufflé. Dried tomatoes give this fluffy pudding a lovely salmon color and a hint of tomato flavor.

4 cups coarsely chopped day-old bread

⅓ cup dried tomatoes, finely chopped

3 cups milk

1 tablespoon butter

2 tablespoons minced fresh sage

1 tablespoon minced fresh rosemary

1 teaspoon pepper

½ teaspoon salt

1 cup grated fontina cheese, about
   ¼ pound

5 eggs

Soak the bread and dried tomatoes in the milk for 10 minutes, or for 15 minutes if the bread is very hard. Use half of the butter to grease a baking dish, and preheat the oven to 350 degrees F.

In a small bowl, combine together the sage, rosemary, pepper, and salt. Squeeze the milk out of the bread and tomato mixture and set the milk aside.

Layer the baking dish with the bread, a sprinkling of the herb mixture, and the cheese. Repeat the layering 3 or 4 times. Add the eggs to the milk, beat well, and pour over the bread.

Dot the top of the pudding with the remaining butter and bake for 45 minutes until crust is golden brown and juices are bubbling up around the edges. This is a pleasing dish served either hot or warm.

SERVES 6 TO 8.

Dried Tomato Fettuccine

Pale orange with tiny dots of red, this easy-to-make fresh pasta is rich with the concentrated taste of dried tomatoes. Try tossing it with a fruity olive oil, bits of steamed broccoli, fresh English peas, and snow peas and topping with freshly grated Parmesan cheese and black pepper for a worthy party dish.

Boil the tomatoes in the water until soft, about 15 to 20 minutes. Drain any excess water and puree the tomatoes in a food processor or blender. Add the flour and salt. Add the eggs one at a time and mix until a dough ball forms, about 5 to 7 minutes.

1 1/2 cups dried tomatoes
1 cup water
3 1/2 to 4 cups all-purpose flour
1 1/2 teaspoons salt
3 to 4 large eggs

Remove the dough and knead vigorously on a floured board until dough becomes smooth, about 7 minutes. Form into a ball and let chill for 1 hour. Roll out the pasta until about 1/8 inch thick and slice into 1/2-inch-wide strips, or use a pasta-making machine. Bring a large pot of water to boil. Add the pasta and cook until tender, about 3 to 5 minutes. Serve with your favorite sauce.

Serves 4.

Dried Tomato

AND FRESH SAGE BISCUITS

Marbled throughout with orange streaks of dried tomato and fragrant with the aroma of fresh sage, these flaky, buttery biscuits are perfect for soaking up gravy or smothering with butter.

Preheat oven to 400 degrees F.

In a small bowl, combine the tomatoes with the milk and let stand for 20 minutes. In a mixing bowl, combine the flour, baking powder, and salt. Cut ⅓ cup of the butter into the flour with a pastry cutter or two knives until the mixture forms pea-sized crumbs. Stir in the sage and the milk and tomatoes. The dough will be soft but not sticky.

Grease a large cookie sheet with about 1 teaspoon of the remaining butter and melt the rest over low heat. Place the dough onto a floured board and knead for 2 to 3 minutes. Roll out to a thickness of about ½ inch. Using a 2-inch-round cookie cutter, the rim of a glass, or a biscuit cutter, cut out the biscuits.

Place the biscuits on the cookie sheet about ½ inch apart and baste with the melted butter. Bake at 400 degrees F for 10 to 12 minutes, or until golden brown.

15 dried tomatoes, coarsely chopped
1 cup milk
2 cups all-purpose flour
3 teaspoons baking powder
½ teaspoon salt
1 stick unsalted butter
3 tablespoons chopped fresh sage

MAKES 14 TO 16 BISCUITS.

Dried Tomato

AND PECAN CORN MUFFINS

The tartness of dried tomatoes combined with the crunch of pecans creates a delicious sweet and savory taste sensation. Serve these moist and fluffy treats with brunch or at dinner in place of bread or biscuits.

2 tablespoons unsalted butter, softened

¼ cup sugar

1 egg

1 cup milk

1 cup flour

¾ cup yellow corn meal

4 teaspoons baking powder

¼ teaspoon salt

10 oil-packed dried tomatoes, finely
    chopped

¾ cup pecans, coarsely chopped

Preheat oven to 350 degrees F.

In a mixing bowl, cream together the butter, sugar, and egg until smooth. Add the milk and mix well. In a separate mixing bowl combine the flour, corn meal, baking powder, and salt and mix well. Using an electric beater at a medium speed, combine the flour mixture with the butter mixture until just blended. Fold in the dried tomatoes and chopped pecans. Spoon batter into a greased muffin pan. Bake for 25 minutes until knife inserted comes out clean.

MAKES 12 MUFFINS.

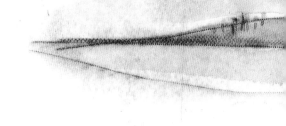

Sauces, Spreads, and Dressings

Dressing of Yogurt,

CUCUMBER, AND DRIED TOMATOES

Full-bodied yogurt makes this dressing so substantive that you may want to spoon it up like a hearty soup. If you can resist eating it the moment this dressing is made, serve it over a salad of cucumbers and red onions or as a dip for crisp, raw vegetables. Any of the dried specialty tomatoes can be used as a substitute for the Red Roma in this dressing.

Combine all the ingredients in a food processor. Blend until creamy. Serve chilled.

MAKES ABOUT 1½ CUPS.

8 ounces plain yogurt, preferably rich
    and creamy
1 medium cucumber, peeled and
    chopped
¼ teaspoon salt
½ teaspoon freshly ground pepper
8 halves oil-packed dried tomatoes,
    finely chopped

Dried Tomato

AND CUMIN MARINADE

*This versatile marinade imparts its flavor to seafood, meats, and vegetables alike.
Keep a jar of it on hand in the refrigerator so that you can whip up an elegant dish, like marinated
stirfried shrimp, on short notice.*

In a small bowl, soak the dried tomatoes in the lemon juice for about 10 minutes. Mix in the remaining ingredients. This marinade will keep for up to 3 to 4 days in the refrigerator.

MAKES ABOUT ½ CUP.

3 dried tomatoes, minced
¼ cup fresh lemon juice, about
    1 lemon
½ teaspoon ground cumin
1 teaspoon pasilla chili powder
    (paprika or cayenne pepper can
    be substituted)
¼ teaspoon salt

Mascarpone Spread

This lush spread may be used as a sandwich filling, as a topping for steamed vegetables like fresh green beans, carrots, or new potatoes, or on garlic toasts served as an appetizer.

6 dried tomatoes, minced

¼ cup boiling water

½ cup Mascarpone cheese

¼ cup finely chopped fresh Italian
    parsley

¼ teaspoon salt

Rehydrate the dried tomatoes in the boiling water until all the water has been absorbed and the tomatoes are soft, about 15 minutes. Combine the Mascarpone and parsley with a fork until well blended. Add the tomatoes and salt and continue to work the mixture until it has fully taken on the reddish color of the tomatoes. Serve with slices of fresh bread.

MAKES ½ CUP.

Dried Tomato, Black Olive,

AND ROASTED GARLIC TAPENADE

This tapenade is a rich blend of three distinct and robust flavors. It makes a quick appetizer when spread generously onto thin baguette slices and garnished with a leaf of parsley.

Preheat oven to 350 degrees F.

Brush the head of garlic with the 1 tablespoon of olive oil and place it in a roasting dish just large enough to hold it. Bake for 35 minutes, until soft. Check often to be careful that it doesn't burn.

Remove the garlic from the oven and let cool. The cloves will slip out of their peels easily. Combine the olives, tomatoes, roasted garlic, salt, and pepper in a food processor or blender and blend until smooth. Slowly add the ¼ cup olive oil while continuing to blend. Serve on toast or with bread.

MAKES 1 CUP.

1 small head of garlic
1 tablespoon, plus ¼ cup olive oil
1 cup pitted black olives
8 oil-packed dried tomatoes
¼ teaspoon salt
1 teaspoon freshly ground black pepper

Fresh Rosemary Grill Sauce

This aromatic grill sauce is full of the essence of the Mediterranean, and it matches well with the favorite vegetables of that region—eggplant, zucchini squash, and sweet peppers. When brushed with the sauce and grilled, chicken breasts, pork chops, and even turkey take on a Mediterranean flavor. This sauce is best made a day ahead to allow the flavors to blend.

1 heaping tablespoon minced fresh
    rosemary
1 clove garlic, minced
6 to 8 oil-packed dried tomatoes,
    minced, about 2 tablespoons
1/2 to 2/3 cup olive oil
1/2 teaspoon salt
1/2 teaspoon freshly cracked pepper

Put all ingredients in a jar, cover tightly and shake well. Refrigerate and let stand overnight. This sauce will keep in the refrigerator for up to three months.

MAKES 1/2 PINT.

Dried Tomato

AND TARRAGON VINAIGRETTE

The assertive flavors of dried tomatoes and fresh tarragon blend together perfectly with balsamic vinegar and olive oil to make a vinaigrette that is ideal on a warm salad of escarole, frisée, and bacon. Here, the sweet Early Girl dried tomato is a delicious substitute for the dried Red Roma.

Soak the dried tomatoes in the vinegar for 10 minutes. Purée in a food processor, adding the olive oil and tarragon. This vinaigrette will keep for up to a week in the refrigerator.

MAKES ⅓ CUP.

3 dried tomatoes, minced
2 tablespoons balsamic vinegar
4 tablespoons olive oil
1 teaspoon minced fresh tarragon

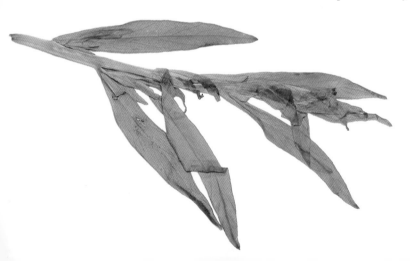

Index

Table of Equivalents

The exact equivalents in the following tables have been rounded for convenience.

Oven Temperatures

F.	Celsius	Gas
250	120	½
275	140	1
300	150	2
325	160	3
350	180	4
375	190	5
400	200	6
425	220	7
450	230	8
475	240	9
500	260	10

Liquids

US	Metric	UK
2 tbl	30 ml	1 fl oz
¼ cup	60 ml	2 fl oz
⅓ cup	80 ml	3 fl oz
½ cup	125 ml	4 fl oz
⅔ cup	160 ml	5 fl oz
¾ cup	180 ml	6 fl oz
1 cup	250 ml	8 fl oz
1½ cups	375 ml	12 fl oz
2 cups	500 ml	16 fl oz
4 cups/1 qt	1 liter	32 fl oz

US/UK

oz = ounce
lb = pound
in = inch
ft = foot
tbl = tablespoon
fl oz = fluid ounce

Metric

g = gram
kg = kilogram
mm = millimeter
cm = centimeter
ml = milliliter
l = liter

Weights

US/UK	Metric	US/UK	Metric
1 oz	30 g	10 oz	315 g
2 oz	60 g	12 oz (¼ lb)	375 g
3 oz	90 g	14 oz	440 g
4 oz (¼ lb)	125 g	16 oz (1 lb)	500 g
5 oz (⅓ lb)	155 g	1½ lb	750 g
6 oz	185 g	2 lb	1 kg
7 oz	220 g	3 lb	1.5 kg
8 oz (½ lb)	250 g		

Length Measures

⅛ in	3 mm	6 in	15 cm
¼ in	6 mm	7 in	18 cm
½ in	12 mm	8 in	20 cm
1 in	2.5 cm	9 in	23 cm
2 in	5 cm	10 in	25 cm
3 in	7.5 cm	11 in	28 cm
4 in	10 cm	12in/1 ft	30 cm
5 in	13 cm